IS IT
science?

Alchemy and Chemistry

Rebecca
Stefoff

Cavendish
Square

New York

Published in 2014 by Cavendish Square Publishing, LLC
303 Park Avenue South, Suite 1247, New York, NY 10010

Copyright © 2014 by Cavendish Square Publishing, LLC

First Edition

Website: cavendishsq.com

This publication represents the opinions and views of the author based on his or her personal experience, knowledge, and research. The information in this book serves as a general guide only. The author and publisher have used their best efforts in preparing this book and disclaim liability rising directly or indirectly from the use and application of this book.

CPSIA Compliance Information: Batch #WW14CSQ

All websites were available and accurate when this book was sent to press.

Library of Congress Cataloging-in-Publication Data

Stefoff, Rebecca.
Alchemy and chemistry / by Rebecca Stefoff.
  p. cm. — (Is it science?)
Includes index.
ISBN 978-1-62712-509-3 (hardcover) ISBN 978-1-62712-510-9 (paperback) ISBN 978-1-62712-511-6 (ebook)
1. Alchemy — Juvenile literature. 2. Chemistry — History — Juvenile literature. I. Stefoff, Rebecca, 1951-. II. Title.
QD24.A1 S83 2014
540—d23

Editorial Director: Dean Miller
Senior Editor: Peter Mavrikis
Copy Editor: Cynthia Roby
Art Director: Jeffrey Talbot
Designer: Amy Greenan
Photo Researcher: Julie Alissi, J8 Media
Production Manager: Jennifer Ryder-Talbot
Production Editor: Andrew Coddington

Printed in the United States of America

IS IT
science?

Contents

Scientist or magician? Alchemists
have been both. In this drawing, the
lion is a symbol of fire. The snake
may stand for what is being burned.

What Is the World Made Of?

Lead is a dull gray metal, not very valuable. It was once used in plumbing and paint—but is no longer because it can poison people if they happen to eat bits of the paint or drink water from the pipes. To the eye, lead is not exciting. Who wouldn't want to turn it into shiny, precious gold?

For hundreds of years, that was the goal of **alchemists**, people who practiced the art of **alchemy**. They dreamed of turning lead into gold. They did this not just because gold would make them rich, but also because they wanted to master the secrets of the universe.

Perhaps you picture an alchemist as a man dressed in old-fashioned clothing or a long robe. In his dark, mysterious **laboratory**, he's surrounded by colored liquids bubbling and hissing in iron pots and glass tubes and jars. He's searching for extraordinary secrets—not just the way to turn lead into gold but also the key to eternal life. He probably looks like a cross between a magician and a scientist.

Alchemy *was* a mixture of magical and scientific ideas. For more than a thousand years it was an important branch of knowledge in Egypt, India, China, Europe, and the Arab world. Alchemy started with a very basic question: What is the world made of? Alchemists were interested in the study of matter—the stuff from which the world, and everything in it, is made. They hoped to learn what matter was and how the different types of matter blended and changed. Most of all, they wondered what they could do with it.

From the start, alchemy had two branches. One branch was practical, or useful in everyday life. Alchemists who worked in this branch of alchemy explored the features of materials such as minerals and acids. They performed experiments in laboratories. They often made things, such as metals and medicines. These alchemists invented laboratory tools and procedures that scientists still use today.

The original version of this drawing was made in 1649, when alchemists still hoped to turn lead to gold or make themselves live forever.

The other branch of alchemy was more mystical, or spiritual. This branch of alchemy was concerned with philosophy, or the search for knowledge. It explored spiritual questions, even magical ideas. Some of the alchemists in this branch did not spend much time in the laboratory. They were more interested in studying old writings and looking for clues to cosmic mysteries, such as whether it was possible for a human being to become perfect or to live forever.

In some times and places, the practical side of alchemy was stronger. In the eight and ninth centuries, for example, alchemists in the Islamic world of the Middle East took a scientific approach to their work. In other times and places, the spiritual side had more influence. Many European alchemists of the fifteenth, sixteenth, and seventeenth centuries saw alchemy as a path to enlightenment or mystical knowledge.

Eventually, though, the two branches of alchemy split apart. The spiritual and mystical side fell out of popularity, for the most part. People began to see it as a form of **superstition**, or **pseudoscience**—something with no real basis in fact.

But the practical side of alchemy did not fade away. Instead, it grew into the modern science of chemistry. Because **chemistry** is a science, it follows the steps of the **scientific method**. Understanding the scientific method helps us know what is science—and what is not.

ONE

The Scientific Method

Science is the search for accurate knowledge about the world. The scientific method, which came into use in the seventeenth century, is a set of guidelines for that search.

The Scientific Method

The scientific method is a process, or series of steps. There are many versions, but the basic steps are:

Observation

Research

Hypothesis

Test or Experiment

Conclusion

Share and Repeat

Observation means seeing something that raises a question. Early alchemists, for example, observed several interesting facts about a mineral ore called galena. (Today scientists call it lead sulfide.) Galena is made up of lead and sulfur. It has been mined for a long time in many parts of the world. Galena looks like and feels like pure lead—it is silvery gray and heavy. But ancient metalworkers knew that galena behaves very differently from lead. Unlike lead, galena cannot be molded into any shape. If a metalworker tried to cut or hammer galena, it broke into cubes.

Early alchemists noticed that when galena was heated, it gave off a rotten-egg smell (the smell of sulfur). When the galena cooled, it could be shaped, and it no longer shattered into cubes when hammered. The fire had changed the galena into lead—but how? That was the question that grew out of observation.

The next step, *research*, is gathering data, or information, that might answer the question. Maybe the answer is already known. If it is not known, research gives the scientist data that may lead to the answer.

Most of the world's lead comes from this ore, galena. Early alchemists were curious about it.

What about the question of galena turning into lead? Alchemists could research that question in a few ways. They could experiment with lead to see if they could find a way to turn it back into galena. They could experiment with galena to see if something other than fire, such as water or acid, would also turn it into lead. Or they could experiment with fire to see if it changed other materials the same way it had changed the galena. All of these are the kinds of experiments that alchemists performed.

A *hypothesis* is the next step in the scientific method. It is an educated guess based on what the scientist has observed and researched. To explain the change from galena to lead, an alchemist might say, "I noticed the smell of sulfur when I heated the galena. Maybe the heat of the fire drove sulfur out of the galena, leaving behind only lead." This would mean that sulfur is different in some important way from lead, because the fire made the sulfur disappear but not the lead. Therefore sulfur has different **properties** than lead.

Testing the hypothesis shows whether or not it is the right explanation. This part of the scientific method often involves experiments. Even when a scientist cannot actually do a particular experiment, he or she must at least be able to *think* of a way the hypothesis *could* be tested. A scientific hypothesis must be testable. If it cannot be tested, it cannot be proved—or disproved. That removes it from the realm of science.

How could an alchemist test the hypothesis about sulfur in galena? He could heat many samples of galena. If every experiment gave off the smell of rotten eggs, and every experiment also produced lead as the end product, the alchemist could be fairly sure that his hypothesis was correct.

A *conclusion* comes from tests and experiments. In this step, the scientist looks at the results of the experiments and asks, "Do these results support my hypothesis?"

If the answer is "no," the scientist adds the results to his or her observations, then thinks of a new hypothesis. Good scientists admit their mistakes and wrong ideas, because their goal is to be accurate and truthful. Good scientists are also flexible, growing and changing as new knowledge is gained.

If the answer is "yes," the scientist usually *repeats* the experiment to make sure. To be considered scientific, the result of a test or experiment has to be able to be reproduced. Today, scientists *share* their work by publishing it in **scientific journals** so that others can test it, too.

The scientific method is a powerful way to learn about the world. It gives scientists everywhere a clear set of standards to meet. It is also an excellent tool for identifying pseudoscience.

Pseudoscience

Pseudo- (SOO-doh) at the beginning of a word means "false" or "fake." Pseudoscience is false science. It is presented as if it were scientific, but it does not meet the standards of good science.

Many pseudoscientific claims are not testable. They may so broad or vague that they have no meaning. "Gold is the most perfect metal" is an example of a pseudoscientific claim. A scientist examining that claim would ask, "What do you mean

Many alchemists believed in astrology, which is now seen as a pseudoscience.

by *perfect*? Copper conducts electricity better than gold, and lead weighs more than gold. If you need to conduct electricity or weigh something down, aren't copper and lead more perfect than gold?"

Pseudoscientific claims are sometimes presented as facts, but with no evidence, or with poor evidence. If there *is* evidence, it may be statistics or quotes with no sources. Without knowing exactly where a piece of information comes from, it's impossible to check that the source is reliable and the information is accurate.

Finally, pseudoscience is often based on beliefs and feelings rather than logic and reason. A pseudoscientific idea may spring

Science or Pseudoscience?

FEATURES OF SCIENCE:

- Based on scientific method

- Uses reason and logic

- Looks for physical forces to
  explain results

- Testable

- Results can be reproduced

- Published in scientific journals, and
  for the general public, too

FEATURES OF PSEUDOSCIENCE:

- Often based on tradition or folklore

- Appeals to feelings

- Explains results in mystical or mysterious ways

- May not be testable

- Results cannot be regularly reproduced

- Published for the general public,
  sometimes does not meet standards of
  scientific journals

from tradition, folklore, or even religious writings. However, the fact that an idea, claim, or belief is pseudoscience does not always mean that the idea cannot possibly be true. It only means that it is not science.

The scientific method has cast light on many mysteries and answered many questions. It is the basis for all the sciences, from astronomy to zoology (the study of animals). One of those sciences is chemistry, which grew out of alchemy. The wilder and more mystical aspects of alchemy were pseudoscience, but the practical side of alchemy was the beginning of a science. While some alchemists tried and failed to turn lead into gold or to grasp the secret of eternal life, others were busy building the foundations of modern chemistry.

TWO

Faking Treasure, Seeking Truth

The oldest alchemical writings that still exist in Europe and the Mediterranean world come from the third century AD, but alchemy most likely existed for hundreds of years before that. The first alchemists are believed to have been craftspeople and metalworkers. They knew how to apply heat to various materials—sand, clay, dyes, and metals—to make glass, pottery, and jewelry. In their workshops, they experimented with materials and techniques.

Historians think that alchemy may have started with fake jewelry. Ancient metalworkers who made jewelry out of precious metals and gems for kings and rich people also made less expensive versions that ordinary people could afford to buy. Early books about alchemy contain instructions for making imitation pearls, along with steps for making jewelry that looks as if it is gold but is really made of cheaper metals.

Creating fake jewelry to sell was a practical business for the early alchemists. But in time, they developed larger ambitions.

Seeking Higher Knowledge

Alchemists came to believe that the materials they handled and the actions they performed in their laboratories were symbols. In other words, those things had meanings beyond the physical level. For example, alchemists thought that certain metals represented the heavenly bodies. Gold stood for the sun, and silver stood for the moon. Mercury, copper, iron, tin, and lead repre-

A goldsmith's workshop in 16th-century Paris. Many centuries earlier, alchemy may have started with craftspeople such as these.

sented the planets Mercury, Venus, Mars, Jupiter, and Saturn. This link between metals and the heavenly bodies can be traced all the way back to 1700 BC in ancient writings from the Middle Eastern realm of Babylon.

Many alchemists, like other people in the ancient world, also believed that all matter was made up of combinations of four basic ingredients, or elements: earth, water, fire, and air. Additionally, they felt that elements could also have symbols, just as the sun, moon, and planets did. The symbol for earth was salt. The symbol for water was mercury, and for fire it was sulfur. Symbols could mean more than one thing to an alchemist. Salt, mercury, and sulfur also represented the body, mind, and soul.

The most powerful symbol of all was gold. This metal has been prized all over the world. It is both beautiful and valuable, and it never rusts like iron or tarnishes like silver. In alchemy, gold stood for perfection and immortality, or eternal life.

Alchemists ranked all metals and minerals on a scale, with gold at the top. At the bottom of the scale were base, or low, elements such as lead and mercury. One basic idea of alchemy was the belief that

Surrounded by the tools of alchemy, a figure called "Lady Alchima" holds the precious elixir of life—the dream of many alchemists.

an alchemist could turn lower elements into higher ones. This change was called transmuting the element. The final goal of this change, or **transmutation**, was to turn base elements into gold. At the same time, according to the more spiritual side of alchemy, the alchemist himself would be transmuted, or changed into a higher and more perfect being. In completing the task of transmutation, the alchemist would complete his own spiritual growth.

The Search for the Philosopher's Stone

Alchemists looked for ways to transmute low materials into high ones. To many, this quest was a symbol of the alchemist's own change into a more perfect being. These beliefs gave rise to the search for the most prized treasure of alchemy: the philosopher's stone.

The philosopher's stone was extremely precious, but it was described in different ways. Some called it a gem. Others said it was a powder, an **elixir** (a liquid meant to be drunk), or even just a piece of secret knowledge. The power of the philosopher's stone could turn base metals into gold. But its powers didn't stop there. Alchemists believed that the philosopher's stone, if they could find it, would bring health, wisdom, and continued life to anyone who possessed it.

But the philosopher's stone was not just lying around somewhere waiting to be found like a diamond in a coal mine. It had to be *made* through a process of refining and purifying

**Alchemists sometimes claimed
to possess secret knowledge and
to have mysterious powers.**

elements. For hundreds of years, alchemists were on a quest to discover the exact elements to start with, and how to purify and combine them to make the philosopher's stone. Along the way, they learned a great deal about the properties of many elements.

Ancient Alchemists of the Greek World

Several thousand years ago, alchemy flourished in the Greek-influenced cultures around the Mediterranean Sea. The idea of the four elements—earth, air, fire, and water—shows up even earlier, around 450 BC, in the writings of the Greek philosopher Empedocles.

Around 340 BC, Aristotle, one of the most famous ancient Greek philosophers and scientists, wrote about the four elements. He also claimed that each element had its own special combination of properties, or qualities. There were four properties in all: wet, dry, hot, and cold. Air was mostly wet but also somewhat hot. Fire was hot but also dry. Earth was dry but also cold, and water was cold but also wet.

More than six hundred years after Aristotle, a man named Zosimos wrote the oldest known books about alchemy as it was known in the Mediterranean world. (Earlier alchemical writings, if they existed, did not survive into modern times.) Zosimos was born in Panopolis, in southern Egypt, but whether he was Egyptian or Greek is unknown because Egypt was under Greek rule at the time.

Zosimos wrote that alchemy is a spiritual practice as well as a science of materials. In fact, according to Zosimos and some other ancient sources, humans gained their knowledge of alchemy from fallen angels who had married human women. Although he wrote about turning lead and copper into silver and gold, Zosimos claimed that metallic transmutation was only half of the alchemical process. The other half was the spiritual purification of the alchemist.

This sandstone tablet of Zosimos and Blaste of Phaleron is on display at the Kerameikos Museum in Athens.

The Arab Alchemists

Over time, Greek alchemy grew more concerned with religious and philosophical questions. After the eighth century AD, the center of practical alchemy shifted to the Islamic world of Arabia, the Middle East, and North Africa. Arab scholars in the city of

A medieval drawing of Jabir, an
Arab scholar who treated alchemy
as a science.

Baghdad, in what is now Iraq, translated Greek alchemical writings into Arabic. They also wrote many new books about alchemy. These writings later had a strong influence on European alchemists.

Many Arabic alchemical books are said to have been written by Jabir, an important Muslim alchemist of the late eighth century. In fact, some were probably written later, and by other people, but had Jabir's name attached to them because of his fame. We do know, however, that Jabir urged his fellow alchemists to do careful laboratory work. He believed that alchemy should be treated as a practical science, not a mystical philosophy.

Jabir wrote that all matter consisted of seven elements: earth, water, fire, air, aether (a pure material that was believed to fill the heavens), plus sulfur and mercury. Later, Arab alchemists added an eighth basic element: salt. Jabir believed that it should be possible to rearrange ordinary elements to create the philosopher's stone. He also thought that alchemy would offer a way to create life in the laboratory. As far as anyone knows, he never achieved either of these goals.

Alchemy in China and India

Chinese alchemy was not linked to the alchemy of the Mediterranean world, which historians now call western alchemy. Chinese alchemists tended to be more focused on medicine than those from the West—although gunpowder, which may have been invented by Chinese alchemists, is not known for its powers of healing.

Who Was Hermes?

Alchemists placed great importance on literature they believed had been written by an ancient Egyptian priest or scribe called Hermes Trismegistus ("Hermes the Three Times Great"). Hermes was thought to have lived around the time of the biblical Moses. His writings, known as the Hermetic texts, were said to contain the lost or forgotten wisdom of the ancient world on such subjects as astrology, alchemy, and magic.

In the seventeenth century, a scholar named Isaac Casaubon made a careful study of the Hermetic texts. He showed that they were written around the third century AD, many centuries after Moses. And the texts, according to Casaubon, were the works of many different scribes, not a single ancient wizard. There never was a Hermes the Three Times Great, only a made-up name that many different writers used to add an air of wisdom or authority to their own writings. The word "hermetic" is still used to describe things that are mystical, occult, or secret.

Chinese and Western alchemists did share some of the same goals. Like Western alchemists, Chinese alchemists believed they could find a way to transmute base metals into gold. They also hoped to find an elixir that would cure all illnesses and grant immortality.

India had its own tradition of alchemy. The craft of metalworking reached a very high level there. Indian craftspeople were skilled at making new **alloys**, or combinations of metals. Others mastered laboratory processes such as **distilling** perfumes, making dyes, and mixing medicines. Alchemy grew out of these practices.

Like Western and Chinese alchemists, Indian alchemists were concerned with reaching perfection. Much of their focus was on changing base materials into higher, more perfect ones. These alchemists also had a goal of reaching perfect spiritual and physical health. In the tenth century AD, one of India's most famous alchemists, Nagarjuna, wrote about his experiments with mercury. Legends arose that he could turn mercury into gold. In India, as in other parts of the world, the dream of transmutation lived on for centuries.

According to legend, the Indian sage Nagarjuna had turned mercury into gold.

THREE

The Golden Age of Alchemy

Alchemy was reborn in Europe during the tenth and eleventh centuries, as Europeans met Arab scholars in places such as Spain and Sicily. From the Arabs, the Europeans got hold of the ancient Greek alchemical writings, as well as the newer Arabic ones. By the thirteenth century, alchemy was established as a field of study among educated people in Europe. At the same time, however, some writers questioned alchemy, calling it trickery and lies.

Important Alchemists

Roger Bacon, a thirteenth-century English scholar, studied alchemy among many other scientific and mystical subjects. He wrote that the practical side of alchemy—experiments with minerals and other materials—was important to science and medicine. The philosophical or mystical side of alchemy, Bacon wrote, had to do with religious concerns, such as saving human souls and becoming united with God.

**Roger Bacon (left) and Nicolas Flamel
(kneeling) were famous alchemists.**

Nicolas Flamel was a French alchemist of the late fourteenth century. He was especially interested in the search for the philosopher's stone, and after his death he gained the reputation of having created it. He was also rumored to have found the elixir of eternal life—which doesn't seem to make much sense, as Flamel died in 1418 and was buried under a tombstone he designed himself. In reality, most of the texts that Flamel was said to have written, and the legends about him, did not appear until the early seventeenth century. Historians think that other alchemists published their own works under Flamel's name to make

Poets Against Alchemy

Two of the greatest poets of the Middle Ages had harsh words for alchemists. Geoffrey Chaucer, the fourteenth-century English poet who wrote *The Canterbury Tales*, let a character called the Yeoman describe an alchemist who used real gold and silver to trick people into thinking he possessed the secret of creating precious metals. He then sold the "secret" (which was worthless) to those he had tricked. The Italian poet Dante Alighieri wrote in *The Inferno*, his tale of an imaginary journey through the underworld, that he saw alchemists among the sinners in hell being punished for their lies and frauds.

them seem older and more important, just as earlier writers had used the name of the imaginary Hermes Trismegistus.

Strong elements of wizardry and occultism entered alchemy in the writings of the German alchemist Heinrich Cornelius Agrippa, who was active in the early sixteenth century. At some times in his life, Agrippa claimed to possess magical powers, but at other times he spoke out against the study and practice of magic.

The most important alchemical figure of the sixteenth century was Paracelsus, a German and Swiss doctor and botanist. Paracelsus tried to strip away the magical and occult parts of alchemy. He was interested in its practical side, especially the use of minerals and chemicals in medicines. He wrote that his goal as an alchemist was not to make silver and gold from base metals. Instead, he hoped to find alchemical cures. He believed that illnesses were caused by imbalances of the elements, and that the right medicines could return the sick to balance and harmony.

The Tools of the Alchemist

Modern versions of alchemical tools remain in use today. The gas-fueled bunsen burner
(top right) has replaced the small coal or wood furnaces once used to heat and melt materials.
Alchemists ground their samples into powder with a mortar and pestle (top left), now used in
many kitchens for grinding salt and spices. Alchemists' labs featured many types of glass ves-
sels, called beakers and flasks, to measure and contain liquids. And no alchemical laboratory
was complete without an alembic (bottom left), a miniature still used for concentrating and
purifying liquids, including medicines, perfumes, and alcohol.

Alchemy in Society

Alchemists could make money by making and selling medicines or imitation jewelry, or by offering their skills in purifying chemicals and creating alloys. Wealthy and powerful people sometimes hired alchemists to help with mining operations (by identifying mineral ores) or to serve as private doctors.

In the sixteenth century, monarchs such as King James IV of Scotland, Queen Elizabeth I of England, and the Holy Roman Emperor Rudolf II employed alchemists. These rulers hoped that alchemy would offer a way to increase their riches by turning worthless materials into those that were precious. These hopeful rulers were doomed to disappointment—and some alchemists were doomed, too, when they failed to make good on their promises of making gold from lead.

It was easy for an alchemist to get a bad reputation as a fraud or con artist. One alchemist who got himself into trouble was Hans Heinrich Nüschler of Germany. He signed a contract with Duke Friedrich of Württemberg in Stuttgart, promising to turn a small amount of silver into a large amount of gold. Several months passed, and the duke demanded results. Unable to do what he had promised, Nüschler saw no way out but fraud. He tried to trick Friedrich by slipping pieces of real gold into his alchemical creation, but he was caught, tried, and found guilty. Nüschler was hanged for his false alchemy.

**Seventeenth-century painter David Teniers created a detailed portrait
of an alchemist at work.**

Alchemy was still considered a branch of knowledge in the
early eighteenth century. Isaac Newton, the brilliant English
mathematician and scientist who is famous for explaining gravi-
ty, among other things, made a long study of alchemy. But since
the seventeenth century, more and more people had begun rec-
ognizing notions such as the philosopher's stone and the elixir
of eternal life as unreal fantasies.

While mystical alchemy faded away, practical alchemy grew more and more important. It was turning into a new, more scientific approach to the study of matter, minerals, and chemicals. From practical alchemy—the making of alloys, the distilling and purifying of chemicals—grew a new field of study that came to be called "chemistry."

A Successful Alchemist

In 1700 Johann Friedrich Böttger was a young German learning how to make medicines. Alchemy fascinated him, though, and he began to search for the alchemical secret that could cure disease and turn base metal into gold. He never found it. Instead, under orders from the king of Saxony, he began experimenting with clays and minerals. The goal was to make porcelain, a special type of fine white pottery that only the Chinese knew how to manufacture. Porcelain was so valuable that it was sometimes called "white gold." Together with another scientist named Ehrenfried Walter von Tschirnhaus, Böttger figured out how to make porcelain by combining kaolin (a type of clay) with a type of gypsum (a soft mineral) called alabaster. Böttger went on to manage Europe's first porcelain factory.

The Rise of Chemistry

Robert Boyle was both an alchemist and a chemist. He was English and Irish by birth, and his life spanned most of the seventeenth century. Boyle believed that the alchemical dream of transmuting base metals into gold was possible, although he never found the way to do it. Mostly, though, he was interested in the properties of matter. He believed that the different elements were made up of tiny particles of various kinds, although he did not go as far as naming these particles **atoms** and **molecules**.

Boyle's main contribution was that he was a pioneer of the scientific method. He saw the importance of clear, logical experiments in the laboratory and of detailed records. Boyle made a number of discoveries about electricity, fire, and methods of analyzing materials to find out the elements from which they were made. His 1661 book *The Sceptical Chymist* (an early spelling of "skeptical chemist") criticized the mystical side of alchemy, as

Robert Boyle's 1661 book focused on the scientific side of alchemy.

well as the trickery. Boyle promoted a scientific approach to the study of the elements. For these reasons he is now seen as one of the early founders of modern chemistry.

Europe in the eighteenth century is sometimes called the Age of Reason, or the Enlightenment. Scientists, scholars, and thinkers of all kinds promoted the idea that human beings could understand the world and solve their problems using reason. Superstitions and unproven beliefs from earlier times were swept to the side. Scientists stopped using the term *alchemy*, which had overtones of magic, occultism, and fraud. They used the term *chemistry* to describe their studies of matter. These new studies were rooted in the old tradition of practical laboratory alchemy, and they used many of the tools, terms, and processes that the alchemists had invented.

Developments in Chemistry

The rising new science of chemistry abandoned the old goals of transmuting metals and creating the philosopher's stone and the elixir of life. Instead, chemists turned their attention to manufacturing new compounds of elements, including dyes and medicinal drugs, and to improving their methods of refining crude ore into pure metal.

Antoine Lavoisier of France, another founder of modern chemistry, proved in 1774 that mass cannot be destroyed by the changes that take place during chemical reactions. Burning a piece of wood, for example, produces gases and ash that have the same mass as the original wood. Chemists of the eighteenth century also gained a new understanding of combustion, or burning. This depended on realizing that solid objects, such as lumps of chalk, could contain gases, such as carbon dioxide. Researchers began to discover new elements in the world around them, and the list of elements that we now call the periodic table started to take shape.

An Alchemical Tragedy

By the end of the eighteenth century, few educated people took alchemy seriously any longer. The idea that an alchemist could turn lead or mercury into gold seemed to be only a fantasy, a mistaken belief left over from an earlier time. That's why it was such a surprise when a brilliant young scientist claimed he had done it. In the end, his sensational claim led only to his death.

James H. Price was on track for a successful scientific career. He graduated with honors from Oxford University in England. In 1778, when he was twenty-six years old, the university awarded him the degree of doctor of medicine for his work in the rising science of chemistry. Three years later he was made a member of the Royal Society, England's top organization for scientists.

But Price was fascinated by the alchemical dream of transmuting elements, or turning one metal into another. He studied and experimented in his laboratory, and in 1782 he told some friends that he had succeeded in creating precious metals. Word spread, and soon Price carried out seven public demonstrations in his laboratory.

In the demonstrations, he mixed two powdery minerals, borax and potassium nitrate, together with a third powder that he claimed to have invented. He added mercury to these ingredients and used an iron rod to stir them over a flame. Price showed two versions of his special alchemical powder, one red and the other white. The white powder, he claimed, would turn the mercury into silver. The red one would turn it into gold.

To the amazement and delight of most spectators, Price's demonstrations produced silver and gold! A few onlookers, however, were chemists. They had doubts about whether Price had really performed alchemical transmutations. Maybe they suspected what modern historians think is the truth: Price fooled his audiences with a clever trick of the hands, the kind a stage magician might perform. Scientists from the Royal Society insisted that Price perform his demonstration again, allowing them to watch closely.

Price tried to put them off. He said that the demonstration was too difficult, and making the powder was too expensive for him to do it again. The Royal Society members insisted. They told him that the honor of the society was at stake. Price finally agreed, and in August 1783 he invited members of the Royal Society to his laboratory to witness the transmutation. Three members came. Price welcomed them into his laboratory and then drank a flask of liquid that he had prepared in advance. It contained poison. The startled chemists could do nothing. Price died almost instantly, a victim of his own hoax.

Alessandro Volta of Italy created the first chemical battery in 1800, marking the beginning of research into the role of electricity in chemistry. In 1803, an English chemist named John Dalton wrote that all matter is composed of small particles called atoms. By the end of the nineteenth century, scientists had learned a great deal more about atoms and how they combine into molecules. They had also discovered radioactivity, a powerful but invisible property of some elements, and they had determined that atoms were made up of electrons and ions. More discoveries about the atomic structure of matter followed in the early twentieth century.

By this time, chemistry was dividing into many branches. Among these were iatrochemistry, concerned with making medicines; industrial chemistry, concerned with large-scale manufacturing processes, including the making of chemical dyes and camera film; and biochemistry, concerned with the chemical properties of blood, cells, vitamins, hormones, and other aspects of living plants and animals.

Alchemy and Chemistry Today

Today chemistry is a broad field of scientific activity, one that touches many aspects of everyday life from taking a vitamin pill in the morning to popping a new cartridge of colored ink into your computer's printer. What about alchemy?

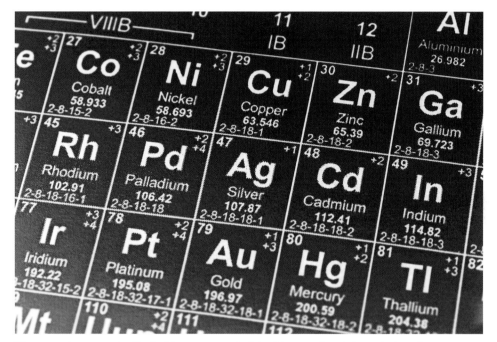

The modern periodic table owes a lot to the early alchemists who investigated the properties of mercury, gold, and other elements.

Alchemy is now most often seen as a subject of historical study, not as an active art or science. There are still people who claim to believe in and practice alchemy, often with a mystical or magical focus, but they are few in number. Most people who read the old alchemical writings do so in order to understand the thinking of those who lived during earlier centuries, or to apply alchemical ideas to philosophical or religious studies. The practical side of alchemy—the realm of laboratories and experiments—has been swallowed by chemistry, which deals with the physical and mechanical properties of matter, with things that can be measured, and not with mystical beliefs.

The philosopher's stone and the elixir of life have never been found, and probably never will be. But modern scientists have achieved one of alchemy's goals: they have transmuted base metal into gold. Scientists have synthesized gold and other elements, or artificially created them, using nuclear reactors and huge instruments called particle accelerators. Scientific transmutation of metals requires a great deal of energy and expensive equipment. Using that method to make gold turned out to be far more expensive than simply buying it.

There is another way to make gold in the laboratory, as researchers at Michigan State University announced in 2012. Working together, a microbiologist and an artist showed that solid gold can be created from gold chloride, a form of liquid gold that is found in nature and is toxic, or poisonous. One creature thrives in gold chloride, however. It is a tiny bacterium called *Cupriavidus metallidurans*. When the researchers fed gold chloride to some of these bacteria, the bacteria digested the toxins and produced a nugget of 24-karat gold. "This is neo-alchemy," said the artist on the team. "Every part, every detail is a cross between modern microbiology and alchemy." Although the early alchemists could never have imagined modern nuclear reactors and microbiological laboratories, one of their ancient dreams has finally become a reality.

Glossary

alchemist   someone who practices alchemy

alchemy   an ancient and medieval science (the basis of modern chemistry) that was also a tradition of philosophical, mystical, and magical investigation

alloy   a metal made by blending two or more elements; for example, bronze is an alloy made by combining tin and copper

atom   the basic unit of chemical elements; the building block of all matter

chemist   one who practices the science of chemistry

chemistry   the modern descendant of alchemy; the science of identifying and studying the elements that make up matter, along with their properties

distilling a chemical process to purify a liquid by heating it until it turns into steam or vapor (tiny droplets hanging in the air), then letting the vapor cool until it condenses, or turns back into a liquid; alchemists used a piece of equipment called an alembic for distilling chemicals

elixir a liquid medicine or potion; alchemists hoped to find the "elixir of life," which they thought would cure any illness and maybe even allow people live to forever

laboratory a place used for scientific experiment and investigation

molecule a set of atoms that are bonded together to form a chemical compound (a material made up of more than one kind of atom); for example, water is a compound with molecules made of two hydrogen atoms and one oxygen atom

properties features, qualities, or ways of behaving; each chemical element has its own properties, including the temperature at which it melts and whether or not it dissolves in water

pseudoscience false science—something that looks like science, or claims to be science, but isn't

scientific journals publications (hardcopy or digital) that contain articles written by scientists, describing their research, and approved for publication by other scientists

scientific method a set of practical steps for answering questions about the world and adding to knowledge about objects and events in nature

superstition a belief or habit that is not logical or reasonable and may even be disproved by science—many superstitions come from beliefs in luck or magic

transmutation changing, or transmuting, one thing into another; early alchemists, for example, wanted to transmute "lower" metals such as lead and copper into "higher" ones such as silver and gold

Timeline

1700 BC	Ancient Babylonians see a link between certain metals and the heavenly bodies; this idea becomes part of alchemy
450 BC	Greek philosopher Empedocles speaks of the four elements (earth, air, fire, and water) that make up all matter
Circa 340 BC	Greek philosopher Aristotle claims that the four elements have combinations of four properties (hot, cold, wet, and dry)
Circa 300 AD	Zosimos of Panopolis writes the oldest surviving works on western alchemy
1661	Robert Boyle publishes *The Sceptical Chymist*, marking the shift from alchemy to modern chemistry
1708	German alchemist Johann Friedrich Böttger discovers the formula for making porcelain

1774	Antoine Lavoisier proves that chemical changes do not change an object's mass
1783	James Price commits suicide when his alchemical claims are tested
1800	Alessandro Volta of Italy creates the first chemical battery
1803	John Dalton of England publishes his atomic theory of matter
1900s–present	Chemists investigate the molecular, atomic, and subatomic structure of matter; chemistry becomes one of the most practically and economically important modern sciences
2012	Researchers at Michigan State University create gold in the lab by combining a bacterium with a toxic form of liquid gold found in nature

Find Out More

Books

Carey, Stephen S. *A Beginner's Guide to Scientific Method.*
Independence, KY: Wadsworth, 2011.

Glass, Susan. *Prove It! The Scientific Method in Action.* Oxford,
UK: Raintree, 2006.

Ogilvy, Guy. *The Alchemist's Kitchen: Extraordinary Potions &
Curious Notions.* New York: Walker & Company, 2006.

Townsend, John. *Crazy Chemistry.* Mankato, MN:
Heinemann-Raintree, 2007.

Websites

How Science Works
http://kids.niehs.nih.gov/explore/scienceworks/index.htm
Part of the National Institute of Health website, How Science
Works is designed for kids and includes a summary of the
scientific method.

Distinguishing Science and Pseudoscience

http://www.quackwatch.com/01QuackeryRelatedTopics/pseudo.html
The Quackwatch site, which points out examples of bad science, includes a look at the features of good and bad science.

History of Alchemy

http://www.alchemylab.com/history_of_alchemy.htm
Brief but fact-filled surveys of alchemy in Egypt, China, Arabia, and Europe, from the seventeenth century to the present.

Alchemy and Modern Chemistry

http://www.scienceandyou.org/articles/ess_08.shtml
Part of the Science and You website, this page is a short overview of how chemistry developed from its roots in alchemy.

A Brief History of Alchemy

http://www.chm.bris.ac.uk/webprojects2002/crabb/history.html
Hosted by the University of Bristol's School of Chemistry, this page traces the path from alchemy in the ancient world to chemistry in the modern world.

Chem4Kids

http://www.chem4kids.com/
The Chem4kids site defines key terms and concepts from chemistry, such as matter, atom, and element.

Bibliography

Cobb, Cathy and Harold Goldwhite. *Creations of Fire: Chemistry's Lively History from Alchemy to the Atomic Age*. New York: Plenum Press, 1995.

Heuser, Stephen. "Good as Gold: What Alchemists Got Right." *Boston Globe*, March 15, 2009. http://www.boston.com/bostonglobe/ideas/articles/2009/03/15/good_as_gold/?page=full

Levere, Trevor Harvey. *Transforming Matter: A History of Chemistry from Alchemy to the Buckyball*. Baltimore: Johns Hopkins University Press, 2001.

MacManus, Christopher. "Bling! Researchers create 24k gold in the lab." **CNET**, October 4, 2012. http://news.cnet.com/8301-17938_105-57526387-1/bling-researchers-create-24k-gold-in-the-lab/

Moran, Bruce T. *Distilling Knowledge: Alchemy, Chemistry, and the Scientific Revolution*. Cambridge, MA: Harvard University Press, 2005.

Newman, William R. *Atoms and Alchemy: Chymistry and the Experimental Origins of the Scientific Revolution*. Chicago: University of Chicago Press, 2006.

—. *Promethean Ambitions: Alchemy and the Quest to Perfect Nature*. Chicago: University of Chicago Press, 2004.

Smith, Pamela H. *The Business of Alchemy: Science and Culture in the Holy Roman Empire*. Princeton, NJ: Princeton University Press, 1994.

Snyder, Laura J. "The Sorcerer's Apprentices." *Wall Street Journal*, January 4, 2013. http://online.wsj.com/article/SB10001424127887324 705104578151610159393362.html

Wilford, John Noble. "Transforming the Alchemists." *New York Times*, August 1, 2006. http://www.nytimes.com/2006/08/01/science/01alch.html?pagewanted=all&_r=0

Index

About the Author

Rebecca Stefoff has written many books for young readers on a variety of subjects: science, exploration, history, literature, and biography. Her books about science include the four-volume series Animal Behavior Revealed (Cavendish Square, 2014), numerous books about animals and biology, and a biography of Charles Darwin. Stefoff lives in Portland, Oregon. You can learn more about her and her books at her website, www.rebeccastefoff.com.